STEDFAST

Also by Ali Blythe

Hymnswitch
Twoism

STEDFAST

ALI BLYTHE

icehouse poetry
an imprint of Goose Lane Editions

*
*

*

*

BRIGHT STAR

Here you are. Unsteadily
shining next to me.

After a long and lustrous
journey from afar.

Okay, little torch. It's time
I got to work once more.

Hitching my constellation
of allusions to you.

WOULD I WERE STEDFAST

In beloved darkness,
surfeited with arrows,

I wheel, unfixed.
Be outside your human

smallness, the stars
want to tell us.

But the night just pours
with the same old stories.

My little *who-did-what-
to-whom* memorial.

AS THOU ART—

I believe everything
you've ever told me.

We'll use it all
to conceive a nocturne

for your childhood violin.
In it someone small

tries to compose a self
while God listens.

NOT IN LONE SPLENDOR

My own composition
is called *Nothingness.*

The notes should be played by
a solitary wind instrument, who flies

in the window, strikes
a mirror, then flies out again.

No matter
that the mirror, too,

is almost entirely
empty space.

I could see right through
this infirmity

if I weren't on such a path
of devotion.

HUNG ALOFT THE NIGHT

Even though you're phenomenally
astronomical, you are singular

and thus cannot be listed
in my illicit *Messier catalogue.*

It's for celestial archers who wish
to part mystery with their quiver

of looking. To find a comet of eros.
Which shifts and shimmers

like someone trying to sleep.
Like someone with an injury.

AND WATCHING, WITH ETERNAL LIDS APART

The lyric address of the divine
will never be ours.

Failing to illuminate ourselves,
we seize what shines.

These disquieting thoughts
are like the dried sea-fireflies

kept in glass cases.
Even after many decades,

when ladled with water,
their spent bodies glow.

With a cold, blue ethereality.
Like you've crushed a fairy,

says one scientist,
and another world is tunnelling

through your eyes
to the theatre of the mind.

LIKE NATURE'S PATIENT

You are in Earth's infirmary
receiving an incandescent drip.

Of departing minutes. I am
bringing you some gifts.

The soft dirt of our youth
and immortal camaraderie.

Two shots
of our highest proof.

An invisible box.
Its inaudible music.

SLEEPLESS EREMITE

This night is full
of uninvited guests who won't

quit apostrophizing.
Good Lord, the unceasing

speeches, reveries, apologies,
formal need and forceful perorations.

Cut it out, Boy! That's me.
Yelping at me.

A hormonal wafting who is
eaten alive by the sayable.

Everyone is asleep.
You. Our animals. The street.

In these mirrors,
I am a clairvoyance of one.

THE MOVING WATERS AT THEIR PRIESTLIKE TASK

Nothing will ever be
our anticipated debut.

Still, don't we seem
to keep rushing the stage.

I suppose the orchestra
is still warming up.

It's partway through
the tuning, and two oboes

are underwater, handing a cup
of heartbreak back and forth.

No one's in the theatre
but us, my darling.

To acknowledge this.
The elemental ceremony.

OF PURE ABLUTION ROUND EARTH'S HUMAN SHORES

Say we're back
at the beginning,

but this time
the gods leave you

in the seminary
of no wrong moves.

The riverine grasses
of your own dreaming.

OR GAZING ON THE NEW

This will be the one where the two
actors won't play their scripted parts.

The man with the poison on his lips.
The woman with the sword in her side.

A crew of scenic designers
adjusts the shadow set.

The lighting technicians
uncross the stars.

In preparation, brooms the size
of my eyelashes sweep and sweep.

SOFT-FALLEN

Aren't we but two asterisks
atop white sheets?

The courage to die is the test
of the courage to be,

says one philosopher.
I might too,

if I were born in Starzeddle
and buried in New Harmony

instead of Port Hope
and TBD.

My little star, we mustn't omit
all that's between.

Our falling together,
appended here so briefly.

MASQUE OF SNOW

The latest hypnogogic
instruction is to pick

up last year's mask
and wear it till a new year

comes freshly through the door
with all the other partygoers

in their relatable costumes.
My mask is made of snow.

The sign for which
is the same as for rain.

Except for the fluttering
of fingers. As we enact

the helixing of time
my expression tries to be

so bright and cool.
Oh look . . .

How beautiful . . .
I hope it sticks.

UPON THE MOUNTAINS AND THE MOORS

There will be no sunrise service.
But somehow, we'll intuit

the billowy sermon.
That we can't return.

We can only revise
what it all meant.

I won't forget my own
hand in this.

How I rummaged
in your black purse.

Whatever I was after
vanished with my touch.

Do you remember that one night?
Cry after cry poured out of the hills.

After a time alone, the coyotes
were conjuring each other.

NO—YET STILL

During intermission
we are meant to imagine

the action carries on without us.
Once, an act could only go on

for the length of a candle.
Then, an interlude.

In which all is reset, relit.
We must re-enter so softly

on our faux pas des deux.
The scene has changed.

But two figures continue
their delicate revolutions.

STEDFAST

In a pouty bout
of astral projection

I have done the manly thing
and hunted you into the stars.

But perhaps your mythical
creature is really hydrophytic,

with scientific internal
luggage capable of

submerging, emerging
and floating. I espouse you

for Captain of Living Waters.
To replace the old candidate

who makes one fear
one's own body-mind

like a hometown.
Let me get behind you.

Let's don the jerseys
for our new team with a flash

of toplessness for everyone.
The blue window

of sadness might lighten,
but don't worry.

About your mortal love.
You don't have to forget.

Flowers remain
of your tears.

Though your reverence
is not for the Ovidian joke

of transformation, like mine is.
You revere movement.

The streamflow wands
its yellow glowstick

along life's tenebrous surface
and you are recording.

The export is memory alone.
Nothing to cause further study

in the anthropology of discard
by outlasting you. Nothing to join

the piles on Earth, the gyres
in the heavens and seas.

All this bright overlapping
of matter, energy and interpretation.

These nouns, verbs, adjectives.
I was once drunkenly controlled

by the adverb, but now I know:
one moves. I will not say *how*,

because you are the mystic
of your own *how*.

Among all this pretty subsisting,
who could know the secret plan?

We are all just momentary
temperature-whences.

With our sibylline sets
of ancestral instructions.

STILL UNCHANGEABLE

Inside me you run a generator.
It has so much currency,

but not enough money
for even a weak coffee,

so, soon we must go
out into the world

to communicate partially
our own understanding

of how we can all continue
to exist. And this, too,

is a kind of love, for which
we are remunerated just enough

that we can continue to live
here together, hoarding

strength in mugs, browsing
all that has happened,

what may come.
Could we please search

dancer, male, ballet,
body, unrealistic model —

and en pointe from the engine,
I'll be returned?

No terms are forever.
I wish to enter yours so carefully.

PILLOW'D UPON

Let me alight
where I am.

In the blackest
blooms.

Tending your posy
of energy.

The only gardening
I do is here with you.

Growing desire
from nothingness.

MY FAIR LOVE'S RIPENING BREAST

Where is that host
who will buzz us in,

sweep us upward
into the bash of light,

pouring blue drinks
into crystal glasses

so we may toast another day
and all that has fallen to us?

You in your flush suit,
mingling with mine.

I keep pressing the glowing
button for morning.

TO FEEL FOR EVER

Every night, a minor festival
of making ourselves known.

A slow landscape.
Our stolen home.

Where the hills
are set about like pillows.

The dog is a system of silence
when he moves to my hand

to ask if it's yet morning.
The cat keeping warm

between us, full of sparrow.
First choruses from the willow,

its lashes still loaded
with mascara.

I am in a good place.
The thought tumbles

from a higher blossom
onto a similar blossom.

A black dress
slipped down.

A star's proof
in its wavering.

We keep practicing
the broken-onto of dawn.

Trembling and ardent
spring flowers.

On one mountain
instead of two.

ITS SOFT SWELL AND FALL

Each new day is cut
from the key of the last.

Microscopically changed
and changed

so the door that flings open
is never the same door at all.

I will erase even this,
try to remember it better,

write it out again.
And so on down the page of us.

If I must believe in something
I choose eternal repetition.

I'm slipping you the key
to the infamous hotel.

With its long hallway
of choosing you.

AWAKE FOR EVER

I moonlight.
As a ghostwriter

who responds to
burned or buried

letters. They all seem
to begin, *Yours, ever —*

*I wish you'd go back to writing
me love poems.*

To which, *You Romantic,*
I must once again reply,

*Just what on Earth
do you think I'm doing here?*

It was once said that to write
any love poem

you must first invent
the poet who will write it.

There is no return post
from ashes or dust.

But don't worry,
I am nearly there.

IN A SWEET UNREST

All this wasted brilliance
we lie within.

Surrenderish,
prone.

In a midlife that finds us
so uncomposed.

Enjoying companionship
with a faraway fear.

Just two animals making
their possibilities known.

STILL, STILL

Being in love
is a lake.

The world
turns upside down.

We shatter it
when we dive in.

How dark
it had to become.

To see the unnumbered
sparks on each shook swell.

To feel their gold
hooks fixed in us.

TO HEAR HER TENDER-TAKEN BREATH

My better angels sing to me
if I don't move too much.

But I am only what comes
instinctively.

I, the body.
The instrument,

the baton, the bow.
The quiet note

of your accompaniment
librates air.

AND SO LIVE EVER—

For one moment
we're held, just so.

By a hand that knows
us best. As though

we're silk stems.
Or a hare's ears.

In the soft grip
of suspense

before we are lifted
from the magician's hat.

OR ELSE SWOON

A winter dawn.
We swan

in the follow spot
of our fabled stage.

A man with a bow and arrow
pursues a wedge of swans

to a lake of tears
and finds refuge, unfledged.

Or he steals a swan's coat
and marries her

telluric nakedness.
Or he's swan drawn,

driving a heavenly
chariot, losing control

of time. Or he throws
down the bow

between the lines
of his indecision

and receives furious oration
from the charioteer

who drove him into
an impossible position.

There are no swans
in that one. Just divine

self-revelation
between best friends.

In one, you play
the young man cured

of his love for another
young man. I play

the other young man
who, enraged, drowns.

Will you sing and dive
where I fell to you?

The gods will so enjoy
your sad songs,

they'll transform you
into a heavenly swan.

In another, you play the black swan,
and you play the white swan,

and I play the prince
who chooses wrong.

To break the spell,
he must pledge his love.

I hope he breaks
his weapon and does.

Or let us both play
Nijinsky — and just keep lifting

the form
with our queerness.

It's a lake. Or a city.
A battlefield, the sky,

ancient fiction.
It's just a stage.

In every story,
the appetent hand

takes hold
and in apotheosis of love,

we drown, or ascend,
or die best friends

by each other's side.
In our immarital bed,

a cloud of feathers is gathering
at our thighs,

our fingers, we open
our mouths and, I swear

I don't make these things up,
clouds, tipped

gold or lead,
one arrow pluming in —

toward one myth
dissolving within

another, risking
our own nihility.

TO DEATH

I no longer commit
apostrophe

when I say to you,
Good morning,

and *not to hurry*
when you dress.

I, too, shall remain
unadorned

but for a dangling
erring.

ACKNOWLEDGEMENTS

This book was written on Land stewarded and governed for generations by Squamish, Songhees, Esquimalt, and W̱SÁNEĆ ancestors and families.

I am grateful for support from the Canada Council for the Arts and the British Columbia Arts Council.

Love and thanks to family, friends, colleagues, luminaries, and everyone at icehouse poetry/Goose Lane Editions who helped me and the book along the way, especially Elizabeth Hayes, Lisa Lewis, Garth Martens, Anne-Marie Turza, Elee Kraljii Gardiner, Susanne Alexander, Ross Leckie, Julie Scriver, Alan Sheppard, Martin James Ainsley, my getting-to-be long-time editor Phil Hall, and Junkets himself. For Melanie Siebert, who enters the meaning of stedfast with me.

Edited by Phil Hall.
Cover and page design by Julie Scriver.
Cover image by Casey Horner, unsplash.com
Printed in Canada by Coach House Printing.
10 9 8 7 6 5 4 3 2 1

Library and Archives Canada Cataloguing in Publication

Title: Stedfast / Ali Blythe.
Names: Blythe, Ali, 1976- author.
Description: Poems.
Identifiers: Canadiana 20230201792 | ISBN 9781773103051 (softcover)
Classification: LCC PS8603.L98 S74 2023 | DDC C811/.6—dc23

Goose Lane Editions acknowledges the generous support of the Government of Canada, the Canada Council for the Arts, and the Government of New Brunswick.

Goose Lane Editions is located on the unceded territory of the Wəlastəkwiyik whose ancestors along with the Mi'kmaq and Peskotomuhkati Nations signed Peace and Friendship Treaties with the British Crown in the 1700s.

Goose Lane Editions
500 Beaverbrook Court, Suite 330
Fredericton, New Brunswick
CANADA E3B 5X4
gooselane.com

Ali Blythe is the author of *Twoism* and *Hymnswitch*, critically acclaimed poetry collections that explore trans-poetics. His poems and essays have been published in national and international literary journals and anthologies — including *The Broadview Introduction to Literature, Best Canadian Essays*, and *Best Canadian Poetry*.

Blythe is a winner of the Vallum Award for Poetry, twice finalist for the Dorothy Livesay BC Book Award, and recipient of an honour of distinction from the Writers Trust of Canada for emerging LGBTQ writers. *Hymnswitch* was named one of the Best Books of 2019 by the *Walrus*.

Photo: Melanie Siebert